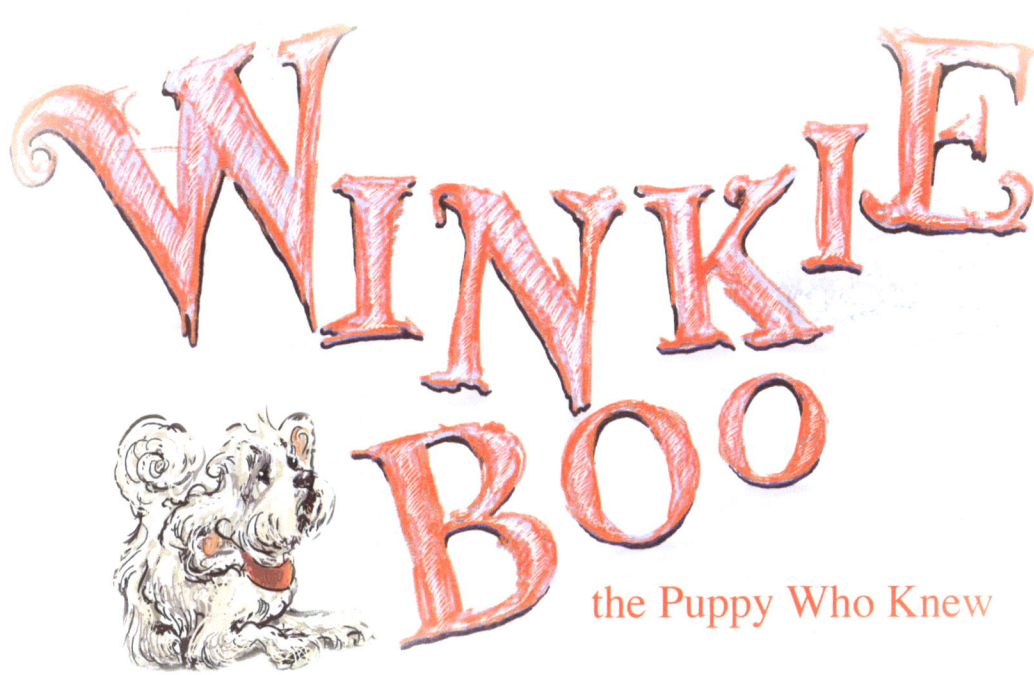

WINKIE BOO
the Puppy Who Knew

by the L. Sisters

Laurie Gourley and Linda Curto

For all the abandoned and mistreated animals; and to the 'real' Gloria who has dedicated her heart and soul to saving them.

© 2022 The L. Sisters
ISBN- 9780984900565

This book belongs to

_____

The floor of the old dog pen was hard and icy cold. You could hear the wind howling through the open window.

Winkie-Boo and his brother Bean snuggled together for warmth.

"I must take care of my little brother, as I promised my mom." Winkie-Boo thought, "But how?"

Light from a star above brightened the broken down factory where a dozen pens held puppies; too many to count.

"Oh, star," Winkie-Boo whispered, "you shine so brightly, won't you please help me to understand people talk. I promise to use that gift for good."

Next morning, Mr. Bitter and his helper shoved all the sleepy puppies into the back of a dirty truck.

Suddenly Winkie Boo realized he could understand what the men were saying and knew the pups were being taken to market to be separated and sold.

At the market, Winkie Boo jumped up and down. He twirled and let out a big "Ahh Wooo!"

A little boy heard him and ran over to see what was happening. "He's dancing, Daddy!" said the boy. "I love him!"

"Alright, Bobby," said the little boy's father. "Let's ask him if he'd like to come home with us."

Winkie-Boo tried to talk. "Yes!
Yes! And please save my brother!"
But all that came out of his mouth
was "Ruff! Ruff! Woo! Woo!"

Bobby and his father frowned. Winkie
Boo knew they did not understand him.

"I don't think he likes us,"
Bobby's father said.

"Yes, he does," said Mr. Bitter, rushing over and grabbing Winkie Boo by the fur on his head. Winkie Boo let out a yelp.

"Stop, you're hurting him!" shouted Bobby's father. He took Bobby's hand and said, "Let's go son."

"You lost me a sale," the mean man yelled and threw him in the back cage.

Winkie Boo knew he needed a better plan; and it would have to happen soon.

On the way home from the market, Winkie Boo heard the men say that this was the last day to sell the puppies. "What will happen to us?" he thought.

Just then, he looked out the window of the truck and saw his special star shining in the night sky. "Please help me know what to do," he wished.

Winkie Boo was the last puppy to be returned to his cage at the factory. Now was his chance. It was time to act!

With his ears pushed back, he twirled, jumped and let out a big "Ahh Woo!" To his surprise, a faint "Woo Woo" echoed from the distance.

"Did you hear that?" Mr. Bitter asked his helper.

The men hurried to see what was happening, forgetting to lock the cage.

Winkie Boo knew what to do!

He pushed the cage open. "Don't be afraid," Winkie Boo said to Bean. Together, they ran to hide under an old couch.

"Woo Woo. Woo Woo", the echo grew louder.

The men returned with a big board and slid it in front of the cages to hide the puppies.

"Woo, Woo." It was the sound of a siren as a car pulled up to the factory.

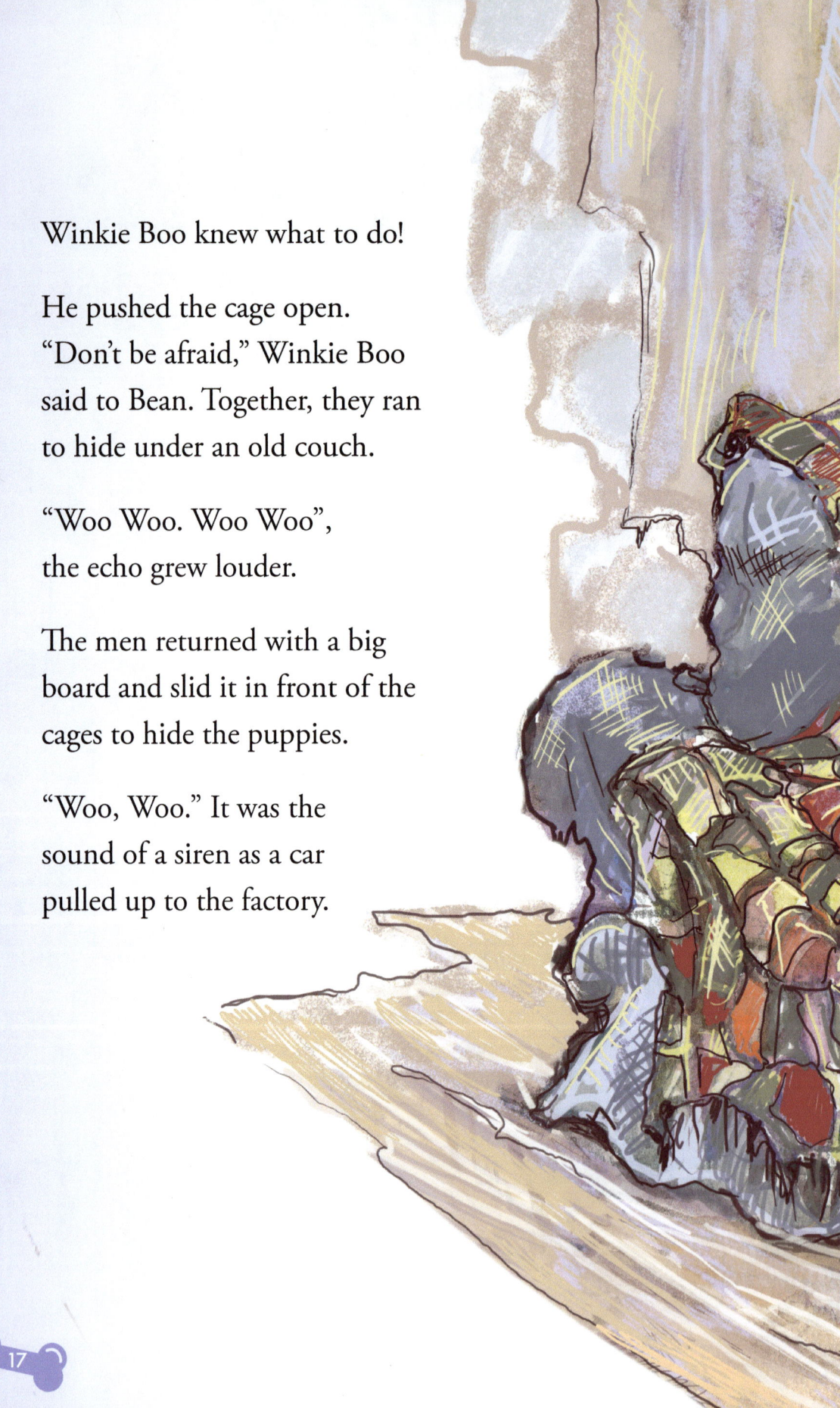

Then, the most beautiful woman Winkie Boo had even seen walked through the door. A star, just like the one he had wished upon, glowed above her head.

"I heard you were mistreating puppies at the market today," the woman said.

Mr. Bitter turned red as a cherry. "I don't know what you are talking about Gloria. What puppies?"

Winkie Boo knew this was his chance. He ran from under the couch straight to Gloria.

She held him in her arms. "Well hello," she said to Winkie Boo. "You are a special pup. You have something to tell me, don't you?"

Winkie Boo let out an "Ahh Woo" and jumped from her arms. He ran over to the board covering the cages.

Gloria slid the board away, revealing the other puppies.

With a burst of joy, the puppies came running out and gathered around Gloria's feet.

"You will never see this place again," she told them. "You will come with me where you will be safe; and sleep in a bed meant just for you until we find you a forever home full of love."

When they arrived at Gloria's they were greeted by many animals.

There was a big pig named Snickers, horses and goats.

There were ducks and singing birds; lots of cats and, of course, many puppies!

Gloria told Winkie Boo that all the animals were rescued from places where they were unloved.

Gloria showed Winkie Boo a wonderful bed just for him.

She knelt down and said, "It's time for sleep and sleep you will, for you are safe. There are bad bits in this world, but know that you have been a good bit in the lives of others."

She lifted his face. "You understand what I'm saying, don't you?"

Winkie-Boo took a moment and then...he winked.

Yes, Winkie-Boo knew.

www.ingramcontent.com/pod-product-compliance
Lightning Source LLC
Chambersburg PA
CBHW042146290426
44110CB00002B/130